FINISH TO THE SKY

Volume Three

MY TEN DEFINITIVE GOLF LESSONS

GREG LAVERN
Canadian Golf Author/Master Golf Instructor

Ian MacMillan
Editor

In Dedication To All The Confused Golfers In The World.

I

FINISH TO THE SKY
Volume Three
My Ten Definitive Golf Lessons

SOFT COVER ISBN: 978-0-9948861-7-0
E-BOOK ISBN: 978-0-9948861-8-7
HARD COVER ISBN: 978-0-9948861-6-3

ACKNOWLEDGEMENTS
FROM: GREG LAVERN

I have never been a person to follow the crowd for acceptance, particularly when my golf knowledge is on an exclusive level that some critics could never comprehend beyond their own self promoted egos. I believe the golf consumer is entitled to the truth pertaining to unknown knowledge and factual information without restriction. I will rescue the vulnerable confused golfer bombarded from mind boggling internet golf tips.

In recognition to my three daughters Heather, Chelsey and Jerica along with grand children Micheal, Zackery, Keggan, Jace, Jax, Jules and Matthew… sunshine, rainbows and lollipops from my house to yours with love Daddy Grandpa Lavern.

Teaching professional Lawson Mitchell who lives in Ormond Beach Florida USA for his introduction of Moe Norman to me in 1974 and continued friendship.

Special thanks to Ian MacMillan Nova Scotia Canada for editing the literacy , video/graphic expertise and his true friendship that continued since he edited my first book in the Finish to the Sky series.

In appreciation to Brian Chambers of Charlottetown PEI Canada for his motivational support while I wrote Volume Three who also took the pictures of my golf swing with his cell phone that will appear in this book.

FINISH TO THE SKY Volume Three
Deep appreciation of encouragement goes to Tim Lynch of Calgary, Alberta a student who encouraged me to write My Ten Definitive Golf Lessons.

Raise my glass with good cheer to the Dowling brothers Bob, John, Allan and Wayne Fraser of Charlottetown PEI Canada for their support as golfing partners and good friends while I wrote this book.

I highly recommend the law firm of Dunlap Codding PC. that has provided me with outstanding Intellectual Property representation from Jordan A. Sigale, Evan W. Talley, Esq. and Douglas J. Sorocco who practice law as a team in the United States of America. Their incredible knowledge of intellectual property law and strong belief for true justice made it possible that the valuable golf knowledge I was taught personally from golf's ball striking sensation Moe Norman would be protected for the golf industry consumer to absorb and enjoy.
Dunlap Codding PC., The Film Row District, 609 W. Sheridan Avenue Oklahoma City OK 73102
1 (405) 607-8600

FORWARD

Back in 1970 my long time friend Lawson Mitchell, a club professional on the Hogan staff, had a casual conversation on golf's future products with the legendary Ben Hogan. Mr. Hogan stated, " the golf industry in fifty years from now will destroy the game as we know it with a total concentration on distance, all the shot makers will be gone." From this quote we now have lighter golf clubs manufactured that strike a hot golf ball to accommodate the development of longer golf courses over 7,500 yards for television media coverage. Money has become paramount from distance obsession for the creation of many new markets.

In the past a persimmon driver took much more talent to hit with the smaller head and insert. The frying pan drivers that have flooded the market place have provided a means to correct error in direction and buy extra yards on your purchase. These equipment changes have made poor player's much better that has lead to a further expansion of tournament golf worldwide before reaching golf's biggest stage, the US PGA tour.

From the lack of PGA and USGA control to protect the game has caused mixed feelings in the golf community. These two major golf associations became puppets to golf manufactures, golf course designers and golf's main source of media coverage for future aspirations to change the game. It has gone too far when tournament golf viewed on television has displayed a deep thirst for distance at the expense of hitting the fairway the way the game is suppose to be played.

Long rough and out of bounds markers is the price any golfer should pay for a missed fairway especially when some of these fairways seen on television are fifty yards wide. Technology has already provided massive distances along with a means to adjust the golfer's club face for straighter shots rather than actual acceptance of a wayward golf shot from self performance. Artificial gimmicks for better performance have become a form of cheating when compared to older technology that demands the golfer to square the club head through impact without artificial club head adjustment.

I suggest concentration on smashing for distance is left to the long drive competition and professional tournaments for exciting television entertainment. The average club player should have concentration on hitting the golf ball solid that will result in straighter shots with adequate distance. The golf swing has not changed from the days of the great ball strikers if you know what to look for. However, a more distance oriented approach is utilized by the majority of modern tour player to plant the left leg like a fence post while the hips spin out of the way so the right side can perform a full release of uncontrolled power. This distance oriented golf swing will allow the golfer to hit shorter irons while paying a heavy price of minimum golf swing repetition and easily prone to injury. The consumer should choose their own approach though I hope consideration of enjoyment and contentment becomes paramount once your own limitations are put into perspective.

Many golf fans I have spoken with seem disgusted with the low scores of fifteen to twenty under par that is made for television in professional golf tournaments. It would seem that six, up to ten, under par would be much more realistic with the suggestion that golf courses on tour are set-up as tough as possible. The reality of changing back to a normal golf ball that travels under three hundred yards is preferred though highly unlikely from all the hot balls in the market place. Great distance along with pool table greens tend to be the major reasons of these low scores though wayward golf shots are not being penalized to off-set these generous advantages.

There is a need to narrow the fairway indentations from tee to green and allow the rough longer growth for any PGA tour events with a serious concentration on major championships. If the industry wants to dominate golf with distance then those days of hitting the golf ball crooked and still quite capable to knock the next shot on the green from an errant tee shot that shouldn't be such a simple option. Toughing up some of the best golf courses for top caliber tournament play wouldn't be that difficult with a different mindset from the approach tournament officials have recently taken. Don't forget the member golf course is only on loan for the tournament venue that would still provide golf club membership accessibility to play a different set of tee markers depending on the golfer's personal ability once the tournament is completed. Can you imagine the PGA tour telling the golf course superintendent of the tournament destination to bald the fairways and cut the rough for more distance.

Also water the hell out of the greens so lots of action can be put on the golf ball for television.

The game is certainly changed. Is it for the better or not?

With the ongoing circus of distance domination that has destroyed golf swings and confused many golfers I felt it necessary that My Ten Definitive Golf Lessons be written with the dedication: To All The Confused Golfer's In The World.

I am hopeful this book will set a standard of reliability to the vast majority of golfers. When your focus has shifted to that obsession of overbearing and overwhelming need for distance just consider when in doubt block out. I strongly suggest that reliable accuracy with adequate distance is the best approach for the average club member golfer.

GREG LAVERN
Canadian Golf Author/Master Golf Instructor

INTRODUCTION: MY TEN DEFINITIVE GOLF LESSONS

This book presents My Ten Definitive Golf Lessons directly from the golf mind of Canadian Author and Master Golf Instructor, Greg Lavern. Throughout the ten lesson chapters you will consume valuable information that clearly identifies, in dedication to all the confused golfer's in the world, the very best of golf swing knowledge the average or advanced golfer will ever encounter or be introduced to. A complete instructional overview is provided from the moment you grip the golf club, with explanation on the golf swing and how to score, and further explores inner techniques of how to manage your golf game. My lesson presentation is a major source of information for the golfer who wants to hit the golf ball straight and pure. I can teach most golfers using the contents of this book to improve their golf game with my incredible insight and knowledge based on perfection learned personally from some of golf's greatest ball strikers in Canada. With numerous years of practice and playing golf with Moe Norman who many around the world consider the greatest ball striker of all time.

Previous books written in the FINISH TO THE SKY series identify this wonderful experience that Lavern has captured and passed on to the golfing world, which has willingly acknowledged:
FINISH TO THE SKY
The Golf Swing Moe Norman Taught Me:
Golf Knowledge Was His Gift To Me.
　　　FINISH TO THE SKY
　　　The Authentic Tournament Winning Golf Swing
　　　Of Canadian Master Ball Striker Moe Norman, I
　　　Personally Experienced.

It would be fair to say that through the years of instruction under the mentorship of Moe Norman I paved my understanding of the golf swing and golf mind that was conditioned on the unknown.

Other great ball strikers on occasion such as George Knudson and Al Balding, who were champions on the US PGA tour, provided some gems of golf knowledge in person while I was a dedicated student of the game. The incredible professional's I was fortunate to learn under certainly qualifies me for a general high standard of instruction with My Ten Definitive Golf Lessons (Volume Three) in the FINISH TO THE SKY series.

With all the swing gimmicks, and golf instructors with plenty of their passed back-and-forth opinions from self observation, have little understanding of how the golf swing actually works which has been clearly shown from historical application. I ask these instructors of authority who they ever learned under that was a great ball striker, so useful knowledge can be passed on to the golfing community without confusion? Its unlikely the majority of golf instructors today could provide a well known name of a great player or ball striker as their mentor.

My Ten Definitive Golf Lessons
FINISH TO THE SKY (Volume Three) will set a general standard of published instruction, this needed to be written at sixty three years of age while I am still alive, for future generations to learn from my golf swing and ball striking experiences of enjoyment and simplification.

TABLE OF CONTENTS

PAGE

XI

CHOOSE YOUR GOLF GRIP WISELY
Chapter 1 (Lesson 1)

The golf grip has two important purposes before the golf swing is put into motion. There is a need to feel the club head for smooth tempo and timing while the unified molded hands simply hold on to the golf club throughout the entire golf swing.

For many years golfers have been instructed to grip their golf club with the tenderness of holding a bird that is followed up by lightly tightening the left hand before the golf ball is struck. I find this strictly for the birds, especially when playing out of long grass when the toe becomes active forcing the club head to turn over quickly that gets caught up unless a tight hold with the last three fingers of the left hand is enforced. There would be fewer hand injuries especially off hard pan or digging into a root with a firmer lead hand that absorbs the shock from being in a much stronger secure position rather than with an insecure light flimsy hold on the rubber grip.

When I take my left hand grip I attempt to apply pressure that feels like a vice grip closing to keep something in place. In my early years I would be strong in the last three fingers trying to draw blood, though I never could. In later years during practice for refinement I utilized all (four) fingers around the grip with a slight turn of the left wrist to the right that allowed two knuckles to become visible. I like to feel feisty so the left arm and hand would return from set-up to impact in the same position with a maintained square club face.

The right hand's baby finger lay's between the first finger and second finger of the left hand. There is firm pressure with the two middle fingers that keeps the right hand on the golf club and the palms together for complete unity of both hands. It becomes vital to cover the left thumb that lay's toward the right of the grip with the right palm. Covering the thumb molds the hands together to secure unity of both hands. The right thumb sits on the left side of the grip that will cause an unwanted active right hand.

If you are sitting around thinking about golf, make a quick grip check to insure both palms are equally together as in prayer to God for the proper balance of both hands. Now you are in position with confidence to grip the golf club naturally with the recommended over lap grip. The consistency for great golf feel is much more pronounced when the hands feel thin and responsive rather than puffy and dead. Preferably, passive hands rather than hands of stone that lacks the ability to feel elastic. When firmness is applied in your left hand, with the two middle fingers in the right hand, this will insure a secure hold. This does not mean you won't have soft flexible wrists with eliminated tension when the hands have gripped the golf club. Don't be fooled by saying, "grip it like you would hold a bird." This can cause a lack of firmness in an attempt to gain speed. When a player finishes with one hand on the golf club, this explains a lack of firmness that restricts the ability to hold the golf club by gripping far too lightly.

The left hand grip is a combination of palm and fingers while the right hand appears more in the fingers. Depending on the thickness of the rubber grip will determine whether it remains in the fingers or appears in the palm of the right hand. When gripped with placement of the club head behind the golf ball is essential that the back of the left hand and palm of the right hand should face the target. Make sure your right palm lines up with the square club face. With a solid grip in proper formation insures two inverted V's located between the thumb and first finger of both hands pointing directly to the right shoulder.

It has been advocated that an advanced player can turn their hands to the right or left while holding the golf club to work the golf ball. I disagree because no matter how well you might play golf, this artificial manipulation will eventually develop into inconsistency. I would suggest if your desire is to fade the golf ball then open up your stance or to draw the golf ball use a closed stance. Your hand action will remain the same where the plane of the swing would slightly change to accommodate the curving of the golf ball. Manipulation of your golf grip from the original hand placement will only cause unexpected bad shots out of confusion.

A golfer can grip the end of the rubber grip under the heel pad of the left hand for maximum distance. However, if you prefer more control then gripping down with the left hand an inch or two will allow you to control the golf club better for more accuracy.

3

Most likely you would be hitting a longer club by using a seven iron rather than an eight iron if your choice is to grip down the rubber grip.

There has been a variety of methods to hold the golf club by amateurs and professionals alike. The over-lap, inter-lock and baseball grips have been historical choices in the golfing world. Therefore, entitlement of grip preference is the golfer's personal choice to obtain the best feeling and connection with the hands. The over-lap grip tends to produce a right to left shot while an inter-lock grip has been known to manufacture a fade where the baseball grip could be either to experience much faster active hand action. The inter-lock grip has been used by top golfers with smaller hands. Formation of this grip is when the baby finger of the right hand inter-locks with the first finger of the left hand. When using the baseball grip all fingers of both hands grasp the grip. This grip style has another name known as the ten finger grip with eight fingers and two thumbs on the rubber grip.

Many baseball and hockey players feel natural and comfortable in the same fashion when holding a baseball bat or hockey stick. The majority of golf's touring professionals use the over-lap or inter-lock grip based on their own proven results. Only a handful of golf's tour players have embraced or experimented with the baseball grip on the big stage in competition. The golfer must choose the grip that is best for performance that supports their hand size and make-up. Remember, my first statement introduced the two important purposes of the grip that you will perform rain or shine throughout your golfing career. Choose wisely.

ILLUSTRATION CHAPTER 1
CHOOSE YOUR GRIP WISELY

My choice was the overlap grip that compliments my mentor Moe Norman who used the overlap grip to win all his tournaments and set many course records throughout his career.

Be strong with the last three fingers of the left hand and the two middle fingers of the right hand. Ideally, you want unity of both hands to hold on to the golf club until the golf swing is completed.

SET-UP IN BALANCE
Chapter 2 (Lesson 2)

A wider stance will promote the proper use of the legs from set-up to finish that starts with a solid foundation while over the golf ball. The wider stance will encourage an aggressive lateral move down the line keeping the club face squarer through impact for a longer period of time. If you play with a narrow stance your hip turn will be longer though the club face is only on the golf ball for a short period of time from spinning hips and shoulders like a top. It would seem that balance is much more reinforced with a wider foundation.

When I set-up my very first movement is stepping widely to the left with my left foot, which is followed by placing my right foot in a position I found easier to follow up from using a wider than shoulder-width stance. The left foot step-out keeps the golf ball inside the thigh and eliminates the ball creeping forward or ahead. If done properly the left foot would be outside the left shoulder. I have discovered that playing in windy conditions becomes easier standing wider rather than narrow. The narrow set-up can cause the shoulders going over top of the legs to quickly for a nasty left shot with weak ball flight into the wind. You want to bore the golf ball into the wind from solid contact that the wider set-up provides.

Nothing should be done at the expense of balance that starts with the feet and generates through your whole body. The entire golf swing extends from how you set-up and so does your make-up in everyday life.

When setting up to the golf ball the weight distribution is between the insteps and on the heels. If you feel the weight is forward towards the toes that is incorrect and contributes to poor balance. You will know the weight is on your heels if you can wiggle your toes. If you can't then too much forward weight will restrict any toe movement that should register being out of balance.

Setting up with the driver the power stance is useful with a slightly closed stance positioning the right foot back an inch or two. Your ball position is off the left instep or heel. The iron's stance is squared up from the five iron and down with ball position in the middle. All your longer clubs consisting of fairway woods, hybrids and long irons can be played with the same positioning as the driver set-up. All clubs should rest flat on the sole plate and never on the heel or toe when grounded.

The extension of the left arm and shaft must become one straight line from the club head to the top of the left shoulder. Different from the left arm position the right arm is crooked and relaxed. To insure this, put a golf club between the extended left arm and crooked right arm to secure the proper position of the two arms. If the right arm is too stiff or riding too high you will know to crook and relax the right arm for the shaft to fit through the middle of both arms.

Furthermore, the top of the left shoulder points to the sky over top of your intended target for easy precise direction. Every time you take your initial set-up simply aim at your target or don't hit the golf ball.

It would be defeating the purpose of developing any consistent accuracy that soon turns into an exercise swing session. For the best set-up with outstanding posture simply stick out your backside with a fairly straight back. The arms hang downward comfortably from the shoulders. Its important to bend from the hips so the lower back continues up to the back of the head with straightness to maintain your spine angle. This must be maintained throughout the entire golf swing.

When the hands are closer, whether high or low underneath the shoulders, there is more reserved power for extra distance. Though you still don't want to become totally upright or the golf club won't be able to follow the proper plane of the swing motion, particularly if you choose to place the club head directly behind the golf ball when you set-up. If you place the club head twelve inches behind the golf ball with the driver and six inches with your irons using a high oval left wrist the way I learned my golf where everything changes in a solid positive way. I am already into the swing from the set-up position and already directly on plane. Wherever you choose to place the club head behind the golf ball it then becomes important for great balance to bend slightly from the hips with either style.

My head position is slightly behind the ball while I maintain a central position over the golf ball, directly within the batter's box, a place where everything must stay centred. I look at the back of the golf ball with my longer clubs and under the golf ball with my irons. The left eye will focus on the back of the golf ball.

9

I never allow the left eye to move forward past the golf ball while maintaining that focus through impact and beyond, that keeps you in the batter's box.

A well balanced set-up is the key to playing good golf. If you don't start off with sound fundamentals your likely to develop other problems as you pursue the rest of the entire golf swing. Now that I have provided my best direction for set-up in balance we are ready to move forward with confidence on the backswing.

Furthermore, the top of the left shoulder points to the sky over top of your intended target for easy precise direction. Every time you take your initial set-up simply aim at your target or don't hit the golf ball. It would be defeating the purpose of developing any consistent accuracy that soon turns into an exercise swing session. For the best set-up with outstanding posture simply stick out your backside with a fairly straight back. The arms hang downward comfortably from the shoulders. Its important to bend from the hips so the lower back continues up to the back of the head with straightness to maintain your spine angle. This must be maintained throughout the entire golf swing.

When the hands are closer, whether high or low underneath the shoulders, there is more reserved power for extra distance. Though you still don't want to become totally upright or the golf club won't be able to follow the proper plane of the swing motion, particularly if you choose to place the club head directly behind the golf ball when you set-up.

If you place the club head twelve inches behind the golf ball with the driver and six inches with your irons using a high oval left wrist the way I learned my golf where everything changes in a solid positive way. I am already into the swing from the set-up position and already directly on plane. Wherever you choose to place the club head behind the golf ball it then becomes important for great balance to bend slightly from the hips with either style.

My head position is slightly behind the ball while I maintain a central position over the golf ball, directly within the batter's box, a place where everything must stay centred. I look at the back of the golf ball with my longer clubs and under the golf ball with my irons. The left eye will focus on the back of the golf ball. I never allow the left eye to move forward past the golf ball while maintaining that focus through impact and beyond, that keeps you in the batter's box.

A well balanced set-up is the key to playing good golf. If you don't start off with sound fundamentals your likely to develop other problems as you pursue the rest of the entire golf swing. Now that I have provided my best direction for set-up in balance we are ready to move forward with confidence on the backswing.

ILLUSTRATION CHAPTER 2
SET-UP IN BALANCE

Top Of Left Shoulder Points At The Target While The Right Arm Is Relaxed Under The Left. A solid foundation that supports a balanced body is where it all starts. Never hit a golf shot at the expense of poor balance. The proper balance will have a great impact on the direction and ball flight. Searching for other faults beyond the set-up are minimized since set-up In Balance dictates the quality of motion that follows.

THE BACKSWING THAT PUTS YOU ON PLANE
CHAPTER 3 (LESSON 3)

When the left arm goes across the chest on the take-a-way there is a feeling that the back of the left palm pushes away for the first six inches with continuation of total left wrist rotation to the right. Once the arm moves across the chest, for a fuller backswing allow the top of the left shoulder to rub as it moves under the chin. The arms and shoulders rotate around my neck being the centred stationary hub. A combination of both hips and shoulders turn smoothly together as a package deal. The right hip turns out of the way while the weight remains inside the right thigh and instep. As the left knee turns inward toward the ball as you pivot the full weight distribution takes place on the backswing with ground pressure to the right heel.

Once a fully coiled body motion is created the club head will work to the inside for a powerful hitting position. The left arm pressed across the chest automatically puts the golfer in a great position at the top of the swing. This important mechanic controls the backswing that results in a full coil of shoulders and hips. Now all the artificial opinions and confusion over the years can be dismissed on how the backswing is actually executed. Your left arm remains straight with no tension while the right elbow folds in tight pointing to the ground or more angled inwards since you don't want the right elbow flying outward behind you. Once the shoulders are turned completely you must hold them back to allow a slight pause for a proper change of direction in preparation for the larger leg muscles to do their job separate from the shoulders.

At the top of the backswing the right palm is under the shaft like a waiter holding a tray with a balanced right hand. Positioning of the left palm is on top of the right with the left thumb under the shaft.

Whether you have a fast backswing or a slow one shouldn't restrict your tempo flowing at seventy to eighty percent out of one hundred percent when going full out. Natural ability plays a big part that performs best with smooth tempo to coordinate the backswing to your change of direction as you shift gears for an effective transition. The backswing is a one piece motion where the left arm across the chest keeps the golfer connected with the natural breakage of the wrists as the shoulders continue turning to complete the backswing. Never lift or drag the club away to start the backswing, now educated with the proper knowledge that the left arm and hand turns the golf club away forming a natural backswing extension. If your choice is to set the club head twelve inches behind the golf ball you still must take the club back with the left arm and hand with a bonus start that you are already into the take-away. Starting the club head behind the golf ball eliminates any picking up action completely that is more likely to happen to the golfer that addresses the golf ball much closer.

The length of the golf swing may differ from the stature and body shape of various golfers while the fundamentals of the backswing don't change. A taller player usually will have a more upright backswing plane compared to the shorter golfer that has a much flatter backswing plane. Try to keep the golf swing long by swinging within your own elastic capabilities.

The importance is to secure relaxed hands positioned at the top of the backswing. Remember, the backswing does not hit the golf ball. Once the change of direction takes place is where accumulation of reserved power. This is why the shorter golfer hits the golf ball incredible distances with smooth centrifugal force keeping up with the taller golfer who has a bigger arc and gives the golf ball a ride. If attempting to create a fuller arc, feel free to stretch away from the golf ball as your left arm rotates across the chest. When you use the full capacity of the left arm the hands cannot manipulate the take-away. With the left arm in control of everything going back across the chest insures the left wrist rotation is automatic as arm and wrist stay connected for movement together in one piece.

If you follow and secure my backswing motion you will be right on the proper swing plane and never have to worry about looking over your shoulder to check if on swing plane again. Let us move on with a change of direction that I will explain in our next lesson.

ILLUSTRATION CHAPTER 3
THE BACKSWING THAT PUTS YOU ON PLANE

On the backswing allow the left arm to rotate across the chest that will keep you on the backswing plane regardless of your size or statue. Stretch back until the top of the left shoulder rubs the chin. When the left arm goes across the chest it will eliminate any artificial extension or movement with the hands when starting the backswing. Hooray! Swing Plane Perfection.

CHANGE OF DIRECTION
CHAPTER 4 (LESSON 4)

The transition from the completion of the backswing to the downswing when it takes place is known as the change of direction or the crossroads of golf. The terminology I usually use is the vertical drop since the change of direction causes a drop of the hands and arms in behind the right shoulder which is "vertical." When the transition of reserved power takes place the golf club is dropped on an entirely different plane from the plane of the backswing. The club head is re-routed much lower into the hitting area that returns back on the original plane from the shoulder rotation on the follow through. The lower the drop the better, this will result from the club face staying on the golf ball for a longer period of time. Low and long forcing the square club face to hit through the golf ball. This will eliminate any steepness or stoppage at the golf ball for a late release.

There is a certain amount of drop vertically from just shifting weight from the right foot to the left foot. However, this is not enough to create the lead and lag you are looking for when the legs lead and the hands and arms lag. The more lag you can create will establish both accuracy and distance. The club head will always catch up to square if the body continues moving into impact and beyond. It becomes essential for the left arm to move vertically downwards in behind you. The left palm facing down from the top of the backswing goes vertically toward the right heel. This aggressive move becomes a result and natural reaction that is automatic when the lower body weight shift starts.

As the golf club is still going back, this causes a chain reaction from ground pressure of weight shift to the left side or foot, sinking the left arm and hands vertically downward.

There is no extra effort necessary other than the perfection of timing to achieve the vertical drop that is part and parcel of the proper sequence of motion in the golf swing. Granted, this is a tough one to grasp for eventually feeling forward lateral movement while the golf club is still going back in the backswing. The hands do reach parallel at the top of the backswing even though the feeling is lower body movement going one way while the hands and arms are going on an opposite path while staying centered over the golf ball. After all, this only happens for a split second when the transition takes place. The plane of the golf swing must change in order to build up lag that will create club head speed for maximum distance and positioning of accurate club face delivery once the club head returns back on the original plane.

If you consider yourself a student of the game and have examined some of the top tour players with exceptional vertical drops who continue to drive laterally down the line for a long period of time will display accuracy with more than adequate distance. There is also the rip-it style player with a fair vertical drop that strives for distance while accuracy unfortunately becomes secondary. The longer less accurate tour player prefers club face on the golf ball for a very short period of time that results from spinning the left hip out of the way very quickly.

Sometimes both approaches click as a combination of accuracy and maximum distance. There are times when these world class players are all over the golf course from missing the wide fairways by many yards. The inaccurate driving sticks out like a sore thumb of wayward drives on other fairways or even stadiums, expecting a free drop when behind an immoveable obstruction. These types of performances clearly displays that something is seriously wrong with the golf instruction particularly at the highest level of the game. Numerous fine players that can put the numbers on the board with low scores still can't hit the driver straight on a consistent basis. It would seem their golf instructors don't really understand the golf swing at the expert level they are claiming. I say this in defence against many foolish statements advocated on television and the internet with the indisputable poor accuracy results for hitting the golf ball straight down the fairway. With the best of equipment, head doctors, therapists and ongoing daily golf practice tells me today's golf instruction has seriously depreciated. Real knowledge on the golf swing has been covered up by artificial opinions on both the internet and television. I offer the knowledgeable golfer or student of the game to learn the actual way the golf swing works as that clearly demonstrated in the FINISH TO THE SKY series. As for the beginner or average player it would seem golf instruction from self observation and technological equipment changes have attempted to dominate the social media. The message I get when money is put ahead of sport is, simply, the heck with the way this great game was supposed to be played.

There have been few players throughout the history of golf that can repeat their golf swing or have demonstrated pure ball striking by consistently hitting the fairway or fifteen to eighteen greens every round. The older players have demonstrated much better, consistent ball striking results than the majority of tour players today. There is a handful playing professional golf with top notch ball striking while the rest of the competitors must rely on an exceptional short game to cover up for poorly hit tee shots. Historically the shorter golf courses demanded accurate shot making while the longer courses require distance as a priority to have an opportunity to score. This is why the style of the modern player during the downswing differs from the older player and the golf instruction today demonstrates a distance oriented approach. There is no right or wrong approach when it comes to achieving the final result to score. Many terrible golf swings have won golf tournaments with the dependence on a marvellous short game. We have to understand that there is a difference between ball striking and scoring.

The vertical drop that demonstrates a change of direction, is the prerequisite for the master move that produces the best ball flight possible, I learned from the best ball striker in the world in his day. From my experience I might suggest leave it to the tour players alone to hit the golf ball ten miles in order to compete on the world stage. For the member golfer it would make more sense to concentrate on purity of technique to become more consistent from tee to green. The member golfer will enjoy this great game much more hitting fairways and greens the way golf was suppose to be played.

There are different ways to hit the golf ball but unless a golfer can repeat the golf swing it then becomes artificial toward achievement for the advanced golfer. The beginner and average player on the other hand expects trial and error when acquiring new golf skills. Greg Lavern says, "You never stop learning if you really want to get better and reach your full potential."

I suggest watching the 2017 Masters Champion Sergio Garcia or legend Byron Nelson who both demonstrated exceptional vertical drops that produce both distance and accuracy throughout the majority of their professional career. Any world class ball striker understands the importance of a great vertical drop. The lower you can remain through impact, that the vertical downward motion of the left arm promotes, the better. This is when the change of direction takes place and the left palm goes to the right heel. In the older days during the Hogan era there were dozens of tour players whose concentration was focused on the change of direction with a more pronounced lateral approach of leg drive that would retain their built up lag for explosive power.

When the vertical drop is put into action it becomes left arm and hand dominate with the right elbow pointing forward toward the navel. The hands and arms retain the club shaft lag. There is a lateral weight shift to the ball of the left foot before the arm speed of both arms generates a powerful square connection and late release of the club head. An effective vertical drop is initiated when the golf club head and shaft remain behind the right shoulder for an effective application of stored power.

Actually, I feel very close to hitting my right foot with the club head even though i never have. The point I am making is, the vertical drop I make is tied with a vertically downward motion that is recognizable especially if you know what you are looking for. This allows me to hit the golf ball from the inside like a major league baseball player would hit a baseball. I would best describe my vertical drop as the change of direction that combines with the horizontal tug for my continued extension. The two combined makes up the famous master move of Moe Norman and Ben Hogan which I have done myself since the early seventies. Next we will explore the downswing in the fifth lesson.

The change of direction changes the plane of the golf swing when weight shift to the lead side supports the vertical downward motion of the left arm and hand. You will want the club head in behind you to retain your power with club head lag while the legs lead.

DOWNSWING
CHAPTER 5 (LESSON 5)

There is a packaged combination of planting with the left heel and execution of the vertical drop that puts the downswing into action. Weight shift moves from the left heel to the ball of the left foot from the lateral shift. Continuation of the vertical drop and weight shift combines to put the golfer in an excellent sitting position with gained separation of the left and right knees. Actually, the left knee will move down the line while the right knee stabilizes. As you move down the line the golf club butt is retained and pointing down the fairway. The right knee will bend down inward as the instep of the right foot rolls inward toward the ground.

Both elbows will lead into impact. There has been historical talk about the sole right elbow driving into the navel or leading forward. One elbow leading is not good enough or complete. It becomes important to lead with both elbows where the left or lead elbow momentum helps to propel the left arm pulling sensation. This will help you retain the delayed angle longer and insure the handle is pulling while leading with the heel of the club head. The result is the right arm and hand will retain stored power for a late release. It would be pretty darn hard to hit the golf ball left if a normal swing motion was put into action. In most cases the result would be a hold shot or baby fade.

I am hitting the golf ball from the inside and certainly not tracing the line on the downswing artificially from directing the club head out in front of me after the transition, which is a total misconception of how the downswing actually works. The proper way to attack the golf ball is from the inside. The lag is retained longer with conversion into a pure strike from smooth centripetal force. Coming into impact the club head returns to square from the position I started at address with the left arm lead while the right hand is along for the ride in a secure position. I have stressed the importance of unity with both hands from my description of the grip. Since the left arm and hand are first to strike the golf ball is why the left wrist or back of the left hand is in a solid bowed hitting position facing an intended target.

Never hit just to the golf ball since that causes the right side to come into the golf swing far too soon. Always hit through the golf ball since the shaft is an extension of the left arm and hand.

When in a saddle-like sitting position the club head enters impact and continues low and long down the line that will promote thin bacon strips rather than large deep divots from a pre-mature release. The bacon strip is a sign of purity while the large divots are a good indication of chopping and slashing from a steep angle. Preferably, keep a low club path for the club head to stay on the golf ball square for a long time hitting through the golf ball.

A great majority of advanced golfers and golfers new to the game tend to allow their right knee to go outward when the knees drive forward during the leg drive. I disagree with this movement as this encourages the right side to enter golf swing far too early.

This is why many tour players hit the golf ball left particularly when they're swinging to the left and their timing is out of kilter. My approach is to have the right knee go behind my left knee as the right instep rolls downward to the ground. Very few golfers would be able to do this probably from lack of exposure. The greatest ball striker in the world taught me this move that became engraved in my lateral leg drive.

Once the hands and arms have started to drop vertically the navel or stomach goes outward to the golf ball and that provides room for the right knee to work in behind the left. This does become a tough position to maintain the right leg in this fashion as I continue with the butt end of the grip and back of the left hand up the line for release in an entirely different way. This unknown rare movement makes it extremely difficult to hit the golf ball left with the right knee positioned behind the left through the hitting area and beyond. Firmly, the horizontal tug that takes place for the sole purpose of complete left side control to achieve ultimate accuracy. The horizontal tug follows the top of the left shoulder moving skyward for exceptional ball flight.

Even if the left arm and hand are continuing up the club path line, they will eventually turn over with gradual progression while the right hand has already hit hard through the strike area as it follows the left hand naturally.

Of course the hand action is different in the golf swing that only a few advanced golfers are familiar with. This is much different than the traditional mind-set of the right hand flying over the left for a quick release instantly at the golf ball. In my golf swing, "I release in a different way" since I hold on longer to the connection of left arm and shaft to maintain a square club face as long as physically possible. I have the feeling the shaft of the golf club is hanging downward vertically from the horizontal tug of the left wrist that gradually bows to the sky.

The great ball strikers throughout history have been known as left side players that dominate with a strong left side on the downswing. Lead and retain the lag to release at the proper time. Of course the right side will naturally hit automatically once the golfer reaches the climax point to strike the golf ball. The destruction of a strong left side through the golf ball is caused when the backswing is not completed and the downswing is rushed. These two anxious episodes bring the right side in the downswing far too soon causing the golfer an experience of the shoulders going over top of the lower body. The powerful lateral leg drive comes to a stop with a spinning left hip that brings the right side into the downswing prematurely. This is why the vertical drop is so important in the downswing that eliminates the right side smash from hitting early instead of a much later hit with a silent right side that eventually releases naturally without force.

27

All concentration should be on left side control during the golf swing as the leader with absolute elimination of the dreaded right side smash until centripetal force has a chance to work. The best golf swings have an automatic explosion to compress the golf ball where the right hand and arm hits with authority followed by the rotation of the right shoulder. Feel the right side is just along for the ride that follows the left knee and arm even though the power source is in the right side release. The left arm leader hits through the three foot impact area with a maintained square club face followed by the natural shoulder rotation of the right side particularly when the back muscles follow into the downswing.

The downswing is a gradual process that increases speed and power leading to a square release through the golf ball. I have found the downswing is most effective when a golfer learns to transfer the force of the strike into their legs for solid contact that will produce the flight required for soft landing shots. The club head speed is generated through the proper sequence of motion creating smooth centripetal force that allows the golfer to compress the golf ball for maximum distance. This can be defined as maximum speed at impact generating tremendous power. When the golf ball is compressed in the middle of the club face your longest golf shots will be achieved. The ultimate is a powerful strike while the left hand and arm stay strong. Hitting through the golf ball with the left wrist in a bowed position with the right hand to follow that hits against the left is the ideal impact position.

If you can train yourself to push off the inside of the right foot going through the hitting area, it will generate more club head speed and provide that extra ten to fifteen yards in reserve when required. The downward force from the ground pressure of the right instep gives the entire body movement up the line that generates into a finished swing with balance that will be discussed in our next lesson.

ILLUSTRATION CHAPTER 5
THE DOWNSWING

The downswing requires the proper sequence of motion that enables the golf ball to be struck from the inside. Your left side is the dominate leader that leads the club head back on plane from transition into the three foot impact area known as the moment of truth.

FINISH WITH BALANCE
CHAPTER 6 (LESSON 6)

Near to completion of my golf swing lastly comes the sensation of pulling over top of the flag stick with the left hand and arm extension up the line. The right hand goes to the flag stick from guidance of the horizontal tug that involves left arm extension with a contained bowed wrist. Normally the finish becomes completed once the left elbow points to the ground. If you prefer to recess as I did for many years from being target oriented then the after effect is to point the club head to the sky.

On completion of the finish my stomach or belly always faces the intended target as the arms and hands swing in that direction. Remember, the golf ball goes where the hands go. If the hands work up the line to complete the finish then the likely-hood of hitting the golf ball straight is very good. For all the golfers that choose to swing to the left the golf ball will also follow. This is when most fairways are missed to the left by the best tour players in the world. Again, I confirm the golf ball goes where the hands go. My left thumb never hitches a ride or swings out of bounds. I choose to work up the line to complete the finish with balance which is a prerequisite for straight ball striking.

We must discipline ourselves to never do anything out of proportion at the expense of balance when performing a motion or swing to hit a golf ball. The balanced golfer that swings eighty percent will achieve control and solid contact.

When the golfer is out of balance at completion of the finish contributes to swinging way too hard with no control of the swing motion. The final result will turn into a strayed wayward golf shot without any conception of where the golf ball you just viciously hit might be headed.

I have found over the years that golfers with better footwork during the down swing are more capable to complete the finish in balance with less difficulty. This is why I have stressed so much importance with regard for setting up to the golf ball in balance so your balanced self could complete the golf swing in classic form. It would be fair to say that you won't have life if you can't take a breath properly. Similar, you won't have a good golf swing if you don't utilize balance first. Balance performed on the golf course filters into your everyday life where you will do many activities much better when in balance and capable of monitored control. When you are in total balance with yourself then you will have the mental ability to control the golf ball. On the other hand when out of balance physically and mentally the golf ball controls your actions enhances a poor posture that encourages a bad golf shot.

The foundation of the finish has more stability when the left foot is flat and doesn't roll over on the side. This enables one straight line from the planted outer instep to the left shoulder as you hold your finish that is essential to watch your golf ball in flight, to develop a finish that appears natural and effective.

Another essential key I found helpful was to hold the grip firmly with both hands until completion while watching the flight of the ball.

How can someone ever achieve these important keys of balance if you hit the golf ball and fall all over the place without a focus on a stylish image of finish in your mind? It becomes easier for the distance oriented golfer to swing for the fence providing balance is maintained throughout the swing motion. Hitting the golf ball solid, in balance, continues through the entire swing to achieve maximum distance. The weight starts on the heels and ends on the singular left heel and inside of the right toe. Anyone that attempts to make adjustments or variations from their balanced weight inside the insteps and on the heels is asking for disaster. This faulty adjustment will restrict their ability to balance with a straight or stable left leg. A great test for ultimate balance is when the right foot is lifted off the ground and the left leg is totally supporting the balanced finish on its own accord.

If the top of the left shoulder generates to the sky, this elevates the arms to an awesome high finish. Complete clearance of the left side and one hundred percent of weight transfer is achieved. When you learn to flow with this movement your balance is maintained without effort to secure high hands in the direction of your intended target. The knuckles of both hands will face directly to the sky, particularly the left one that will remain level.

Balance is from start to finish and continues on throughout all areas of the golfer's entire game from full swing to shorter swing or vice-versa. After all the short game technique is simply a shorter version of the long game. In this next chapter we will concentrate on shorter scoring club selection under one hundred yards.

ILLUSTRATION CHAPTER 6
FINISH WITH BALANCE

Turn to hold your finish with balance. The best way to achieve this is by swinging within your own self at eighty percent. It will become more natural when you become more target oriented with focus on your target and ball flight.

THE SHORT GAME
CHAPTER 7 (LESSON 7)

(Full Wedge): When hitting the full wedge shot it's advisable to maintain good tempo whether fast or slow that will encourage solid contact. The wedge is a club that works best when you hit it with your knees. Leading with the knees is the key to great wedge play. I suggest becoming target oriented with a vision when you first grip the wedge. The pitching wedge or gap wedge are your scoring clubs that must become your best friends on the golf course. My three best friends on the golf course would be my driver, wedge and putter. With all the extra wedges in your bag or available to choose from may require a few more friend selections.

Always strive to keep the full wedge motion flowing long as possible unless your golf shot requires a lower trajectory to flight the golf ball down. This lower ball flight usually comes in handy when the wind is blowing directly into you. If you don't require a full wedge and the gap wedge is not enough then a knock down shot would become useful. There are two ways to hit this shot that I know of and have practiced. Shorten the backswing to waist high or choke down on the grip a couple of inches while you continue with a complete follow-through. For real quality shots with character, attempt to sting the wedge with authority. Don't forget to firm up and become strong with the last three fingers of the left hand to develop this firmness that really works great when playing in undesirable conditions.

(Flip Wedge): If between ten and twenty yards a floater is a great shot on a calm day that lands soft like a butterfly. This floating action is achieved from hitting the golf ball pure with total left arm and hand control. The hands stay soft or passive. That demonstrates real purity when the bowed back of the left hand continues up the flag stick. With this shot I could stop on hard surface greens while other fairly good players experienced many unwanted bounces.

The cut shot doesn't have the softness of the floater but stops fairly quickly with little green area to work with. I believe that cutting across the golf ball with your hands and arms to the left might be an easier shot for most though it lacks consistency. I prefer to take an open stance with a normal short wedge motion; this will change the plane of the swing that supports the outside-inward cut shot with control. Once the hands artificially manipulate the intended motion then bad unwanted shots will creep into your short game for destruction particularly under pressure. The hands must stay silent and naturally follow the weight shift when the cut shot is needed from your bag of tricks. When I hit this shot I attempt to look under the ball for the best contact as my right shoulder lowers under my chin on the follow through while the left arm and hand is pulling skyward with my right ear going to sleep on my right shoulder.

(Chip Shot): For the longer chip shot the best club selection is a five, six or seven iron. I suggest getting the golf ball on the ground quickly for the best pace and roll- out toward the hole. Starting with a tiny open stance with feet approximately twelve inches apart seems to be the historical norm.

I beg to differ on a narrow stance where I prefer a much wider stance when chipping for a more secure foundation. The arms hang from the shoulders while the right elbow rests on your right hip. This keeps the controlled left arm slightly higher than the right arm. My shoulders take the golf club back in position and rotate forward in a circular fashion that keeps the hands passive so the back of the left hand can't break down. The forward motion also allows the hands to lead the club head and let the natural loft of the club face to elevate the golf ball. The club head remains low to the ground for the best results of striking the golf ball in the middle of the club face.

Starting down the first move on the ordinary chip shot is to shift the majority of weight to the left foot. The shoulders continue to rotate gradually while the back of the left hand and arm move forward away from the left rib cage. Preferably, the club face faces the sky while the right side of the body stays relaxed. Similar with the full swing the left eye never moves forward pass the ball while club face and ball contact is made. The knees lead from a small push off inside the instep of the right foot that shifts the weight entirely to a flat stable left foot.

(Bunker Play): From the time you enter the bunker maintain your knee flex all the way through the entire bunker experience. Flex will insure there is no bladed or skulled shots when performing a short green-side bunker shot. I like to keep the blade square when hitting a bunker shot. When using the sole of the club head you'll be able to slip the club head under the ball for a shallow divot.

Take a few inches or more in accordance with the distance, conditions, and type of shot required while staying level without digging. After feeling the texture of the sand with my feet this prepares me with a good perception of how the ball will react. The feeling I have is a spanking sensation when the flange or sole of the club head would bounce off the sand level. Imagine a board under the sand surface with club head spanking the sand where you can't dig any deeper than the board. This is a very consistent method of getting the golf ball out of the bunker with the sound of a thud as the sole of the club head bounces off the sand. Actually, the heel is the first part of the club head to enter the sand. Once you become effective with the golf club's huge flange this will eliminate any digging or stoppage if the sand is utilized as a cushion with a spank. Keep the bunker swing long and flowing. The best bunker players keep the club face skyward so they could eat off the face on completion of their club head extension. Just before approaching the sand at impact it becomes important to maintain the speed and momentum that would avoid any deceleration from slowing down and leaving the golf ball in the bunker.

When playing a plugged golf ball in the bunker, this demands two kinds of special golf shots. Open the blade flat for the short high bunker shot from a plugged position. On the next special shot just close the clubface completely toward the plugged situation. When the flag stick is a long distance away the golf ball will come out low. The golf ball will roll freely with no back spin, very quickly while covering a fair amount of real estate. There is a need to adjust and make accommodation for this difficult looking shot that will come out with ease.

Having a great short game helps when facing tough situations like these that will save some strokes at the very least. Our next lesson is necessary to make the golf ball disappear as we explore the fundamentals of putting to lower our score.

Sting the wedge in the middle of the club face with authority for control of distance and direction. Make the time to practice different shots with concentration on centre face hits.

You will develop a better than average short game if you shift your weight to the left foot and stay over the ball for solid contact. Its that simple.

PUTTING FOR SCORE
CHAPTER 8 (LESSON 8)

From the beginning of time golfers continue to change their putting fundamentals in search for a magical way to achieve lower scores. Many golfers will change to another putter with an arsenal in the trunk of their automobile for a new selection anytime a bad putting round is experienced. Once you understand how the putting stroke really works you can stick with the same stoke and putter for many years with exceptional consistent results. I would consider myself a fairly good putter with the same putter I have used since early two thousand. A student of mine out of appreciation for the progress on his golf game gave me a Ping Zing 2 putter as a birthday present that I still have in my golf bag at present day. The point I am attempting to make is another new putter or changing your putting style when you know putts have been holed before becomes all in your head. Putter manufactures have brain washed the consumer with every wacky creation that money can buy. With exceptional marketing to influence the golf consumer to believe for better putting you need our new putter. I am not telling anyone what putter is best for them or what they should purchase. However, I hope you will open your eyes and realize that understanding how the putting stroke works is all that matters. This will prepare you to putt with a standard putter that also can produce a daily repetitive stroke.

Make no mistake that putting styles are extremely personal and vary among competitors. There are few golden rules that are injected into any personal style.

Bend from the hips in a comfortable position so the putter head can easily be placed behind the golf ball. The putter face must be lined up at right angles to the putting line you have sighted for the golf ball to travel along. Stroke the golf ball solid and square in the middle of the putter or sweet spot for the best results. Always strive to get the golf ball rolling from the time contact is made with the putter face.

Actually, to put things in perspective, I would say the putting stroke is a miniature motion of the golf swing. Greg Lavern says, "A sweeping inside to inside stroke passing square through impact for the pure pendulum stroke." The top of the shoulders move back and through while the hanging arms go for the ride since they are attached. Try to keep the shoulders moving on the backswing and also the forward swing. When the shoulders rotate back the putter head will move to the inside slightly. The distance of the back stroke is determined by using your right foot as a guide. Never allow the putter blade to move past the right instep on putts fifteen feet or under. When you have a longer putt just widen up your stance. Again, never allow the putter blade to exceed past the right instep which a wider stance would measure the length of the back stroke.

On the forward stroke the shoulders will rotate through with continuous smooth movement. If the shoulders stop the putter blade will open with a great majority of putts directed right of the cup. The putter blade moves to a square position through impact and continues so the toe of the putter gradually turns over as the putter head releases. If the shoulders rotate backward and forward with an inside to inside motion the back of the left hand won't break down.

The forward shoulder rotation causes the left arm and hand to move toward the hole, away from the left side. As these move through impact and beyond they will guide the right hand to hit simply because you have two hands on the putter grip.

While over the golf ball focus on the back portion of the ball becomes essential. You listen for your golf ball to fall on all putt's under twenty feet. Listen for that sound while your eyes are still focused downward the same as they were at address. As you become more patient over the golf ball as the putting stroke is performed, it will lead toward more concentration. On longer putts stay focussed with your stronger eye for the first ten to fifteen feet. Both eyes will gradually look left following the golf ball turning over toward the hole.

With your right palm and the back of your left hand must face the spot on the green you decide to roll the golf ball toward with the selected amount of break that eventually will find the cup.
When reading greens the shinny portion toward the cup means down grain, that speeds up the putt. Into the grain requires a firmer stroke that is much slower than normal with a darker green colour. You can have a smooth putting stroke that will not cut the mustard if you can't read greens. This is why the scores are lower on flatter greens. When there are many slopes throughout the green is when the scores increase.

The players today are better putters because the conditions are so superior for scoring. Instructional mechanics on how to putt have only a small impact on the improved putting statistics experienced today.

A majority of golf courses the tour players play is like putting on a pool table. A professional's main objective is to insure the golf ball is turning over with high expectations of making putts from anywhere on the green. There is no fear when on the green that could develop into a muscular reaction of making a poor stroke. Concentration, relaxation, and huge confidence is required to become a consistent putter, that truly combines and brings both mind with mechanics into the development of a really good putter. Most quality putters stand in either a square or slightly open stance while using the universal reverse over-lap grip where the first finger of the left hand wraps around the fingers of the right hand. Of course there are new methods to grip or hold the putter such as left hand low and the claw grip with the right hand as the dominate guided stroke while the left does not break down. I have an idea how these new methods work even though my style is conventional.

Exploring new ways can be dangerous and risky particularly if you are putting well. Regardless, putting has become extremely personal to finish off well from long drivers by a new generation of golfers. All I can say too defend the method I use is that it would require no need to change if you actually understand just how the putting stroke actually works. Most golfers don't have that understanding to accommodate all the mechanics and equipment changes made.

If hitting a short putt you should rise to the occasion with confidence and knock the golf ball into the back of the cup with no fear of missing. Your human, you will miss some attempts which is why we practice the three and four footers till the sun goes down for a repetitive stroke and to build confidence.

On longer putts strive to keep the golf ball on the pro-side or high-side of the cup with dead weight. This will provide a great opportunity to use the entire cup where the golf ball could easily fall in from the right side or vice-versa on left to right putts. On all putts your last look before the putting stroke is put into motion is to visualize the putt disappearing in your golf mind. In our next chapter lesson nine explores Golf's Inner Techniques.

ILLUSTRATION CHAPTER 8
PUTTING FOR SCORE

LISTEN FOR THE SOUND OF
THE GOLF BALL IN THE CUP

The putting stroke is a shorter version of the golf swing. I can relate that the inside to square to inside movement of the putter head in comparison to the pendulum golf swing. I have found the most consistent putters in the game keep the top of their shoulders moving back and through with passive hands.

GOLF'S INNER TECHNIQUES
CHAPTER 9 (LESSON 9)

Whether your target is a tiny spot on the green while putting or taking dead aim at a flag when striking a golf ball requires visualization. Learning to visualize an image in your mind before an action takes place is how consistency of being capable to repeat an action is achieved. You will see the golf ball going in the hole before the putt is stroked. When striking a full shot the flight of the golf ball is seen flying over top of the flag stick. The use of your sub-conscience mind empowers tremendous focus with imagination that enables the mind to play target golf before the golf ball is actually struck. The sooner you can tap into the visual mode empowers the concentration needed for ultimate accuracy. Just before a pre-shot routine starts is when the visualization must be put into action. Counting slowly to ten while the image appears enlarged in front of you will develop the image preparation required to perform the action in reality with identical results. It would be visionary to see a solid drive flying straight down the fairway before it takes place or that sixty foot putt tracking along your intended line that disappears into the cup. This will happen when the golfer's re-action during the visualization experience is put into action.

Reaction to an action situation that is easy or difficult must be performed with balanced emotions of not being too high or too low. Controlled emotions can be put into action with positivity rather than a frustrated approach. Confidence without hesitation is the key inter-action for a reaction put into action that usually eliminates clutter in the mind or any negative thoughts.

A calm demeanour usually surfaces on the golf course when total relaxation of the golfer's nervous system becomes an identifiable feeling of patience. Nervousness is usually set-off from being unsure of the unexpected or unknown. Don't allow fear to disrupt a relaxed demeanour of a well adjusted nervous system. Try to stay loose and flow with gracefulness that helps the nervous system avoid any possible tension. If tension occurs it could cause a jerk of the putter or stoppage in the full golf swing that might send a tee shot wayward. How does the nervous system stay relaxed? Maybe a song can be sung or hum a tune while doing a happy dance before you tee off. Another approach is to think of a beautiful destination that represents relaxation rather than tension acquired from daily activities.

Actually, the best way to control your inner golf emotion is the education of effective breathing. Once you start using your breathing properly, as a life source filters into a powerful force within, for your most explosive power and energy ever experienced that breaks boards and compresses golf balls.

The Mind Follows Our Breathing:
For golfers when you take breath inhale through the nose as you take the golf club back and exhale out the mouth as you're coming into impact. Just below the belly button of the stomach is your centre where your energy and power is stored. This is your Chi. When the Chi is activated it becomes your inner and outer world. I was always taught to inhale the goodness of the world and exhale the badness of the (not to do's) to become clean with a fresh outlook. We should all strive to live for the moment as we would over a golf shot without confusion.

Our concentration during that moment is focused on breathing properly. This is a great way to eliminate any anxiety or stress from clogging the mind.

During my martial arts training I practiced some Zen meditation as a black belt in karate that I achieved in 2002. The true purpose of Zen teaching is to see things as they are, to observe things as they are and to let everything go as it goes. (Let it happen.) When your mind is concentrating on your breathing that will then allow you to experience freedom on the golf course or in your everyday activities with confidence. If breathing is done properly your body and mind become one with purity. Once you have that purified sense you will learn from those around you and become friendly with others. The ultimate difficulty is keeping our mind pure with pure practice in the fundamental sense to reach enlightenment. This is not some good feeling or a particular state of mind. When you achieve what you attempt without a wobbling body and wandering mind, this is enlightenment.

The Zen Mind similar to the golf mind never closes and should be open to everything. If your mind is empty it will be ready for anything. The golfer in the same fashion as the humble martial artist should think of themselves as a beginner. This is the secret to continual learning. Both Moe Norman and Bruce Lee have said at various times that, "you never stop learning where you can always get better." The connection between golf and the martial arts are similar when it comes to breathing and the development of the mind.

When you punch or kick in the martial arts you inhale through your nose from the Chi and exhale slowly or gradual as you make the strike. The Master Teacher's in the martial arts have been doing this for centuries. In the golf swing it works the same way where you inhale through the nose from the Chi and exhale slowly or gradual out the mouth as you come into impact or the strike. This is how the martial artists increase their power and explosiveness. Breathing through the nose and gradually exhale on short pressure putts will keep the putter moving forward with good acceleration and no tension whatsoever on the green to any length of putt. All of the inner golf techniques I have described are the special tools that pave the way for our final lesson on how to manage your golf game.

MANAGE YOUR GAME AS A POSITIVE GOLFER
CHAPTER 10 (LESSON 10)

For top performance the mind must become open with freedom to think clearly in all situations that arise during a round of golf. Learn to clear the cob webs from your mind to explore the power within your mind. It usually takes an idea, goal, or focus on a situation to take action for success. The desired action put into place will require self-motivation for inspirational thinking on and off the golf course. You must have a purpose as a starting point for achievement to be reached with fulfillment.

When action is directed it becomes the difference between shooting seventy five or sixty seven from the goal setting before the round of golf. Focus on that number, feel that number and taste that number. During the round concentration should be on hitting fairways and greens and never think of score. The key is to develop a positive mental attitude in your thought process. A negative mental attitude must be avoided at all costs. Of course human nature tells us that satisfaction maybe different from time to time. This does not mean that a positive attitude can't convert a failure of your off days into good days in a relatively short period of time. I have found a creative vision from taping into the sub-conscience that will inspire personal initiative for artistic imagination to enhance shot-making ability. The creative vision filters from a photogenic mind that enables past experiences to become useful in a present situation. The reality actually surfaces while fantasy remains asleep. However, what you believe is what you can achieve.

In life there are moral facts between right and wrong separate from legal facts between the actual and opinion. On the golf course the laws of nature come into play that determine the management approach necessary to shoot the lowest score an individual golfer is personally capable of. Understanding the physical limitations and combine them with the unlimited mind. A tournament player sometimes is forced to dig deep in search of total confidence with absolute belief that the physical mechanics will get better. With good golf thoughts you will have good golf shots. There are times to play conservative and times to gamble on a particular holes that combine together with creativity to win a golf tournament.

Artistic Imagination presents a picture of hitting a shot that you normally wouldn't strike, by taking a different approach of execution for the ultimate result. This requires an ability to view the golf shot before you hit it with a positive mind-set that the shot is pulled off in a pressure situation. It's almost like painting a picture as the artist for that moment the golf ball is flying through the air. You can choose the direction with trajectory being the architect that controls your own destiny.

This is how great champions paint the picture when everything is on the line. The average golfer in most cases resorts to hope and fear in an attempt to get the job done while the seasoned professional believes in self with a positive mental attitude capable of a confident approach. The champion gains total freedom that develops into self proclaimed power to achieve the desired goal of winning naturally. To win on the golf course should be a natural thing.

This is similar to your walk from the practice tee to the first tee that should become a natural experience. When you hear the statement, "from the practice tee to the first tee is the longest walk in golf" deserves an explanation. The question the golfer is really asks is really simple and straight forward. Can I retain all those awesome shots I just hit and take them to a new destination where it counts? The answer is yes if you believe in yourself and what you just accomplished.

It all starts with building a golf swing on repetition that can repeat at will anytime or any place. Whether those fine golf shots are hit with great flight on an open golf range or a lush fairway surrounded by hazards to break your concentration shouldn't matter once the golfer accepts the location. If your practice sessions are based on target orientation, then the approach is to never hit a golf ball without aiming at a visual target. Now, ask yourself if there is any difference where the physical body performs? Actually, the results should be more impressive since the golf courses today provide the best of conditions with beautiful surroundings.

The long flowing golf swing that feels so free and effortless soon disappears. When you enter the royal entrance to the first tee there will be some uncertainty when not conditioned for tournament play. The negative attempts to overpower the positive thoughts of that flowing golf swing you probably experienced moments before. All of a sudden your golf swing has lost rhythm, becomes short while getting faster. Your new objective is to get that drive over quickly based on hope and fear to avoid embarrassment with your playing partners or anyone that is watching.

All of a sudden the patient golfer becomes desperate and frustrated. The quality and perfection of hard work disappeared once your emotions came into contact with physical performance. A good example is the British Open Championship where we have watched many of the best players in the world finding the left rough on their first swing of the tournament. Full of fear from unwanted emotions that destroyed a golf swing groomed on a daily basis for years at that particular moment. The objective to hit the golf ball from point A to point B with a vision of fairway only, is all that should matter. Sand traps, hazards, trees and rough only come into play when the golfer makes poor contact and the golf ball flies to unfamiliar places in control of the golfer. The need for deliberation must be applied with a developed golf swing to control the golf ball under all conditions and circumstances.

When I use to practice regularly with extremely high standards I would have a tee box and green with a fifteen yard landing area where high grass separated the two. If I didn't hit the green I would be looking for stray golf balls for hours that could easily disappear under the high grass. This form of difficulty developed extreme accuracy since target golf was my only option in these tough conditions. There was point A to point B only. From these practice sessions I took my golf swing to the first tee where the fairway appeared wide as a football field. If I happen to miss a fairway it was only by a few yards with no apparent trouble.

Previously I mentioned keeping the golf swing long with a flowing motion for good tempo during your practice sessions. Beyond this tip I have discovered that hitting effective golf positions is essential if your desire is to become an above average ball striker.

The mind must stay active when not able to practice or play as much as you would like too. The golfer can always practice in the mind without hitting a golf ball if understanding and knowledge is based on how the golf swing must perform to hit the golf ball pure and straight. When a golfer is able to connect mind and body then the walk to the first tee gets shorter and shorter such that it becomes just another shot executed in the same procedure as the practice session.

Freedom is power. When you allow yourself to remain free for performance which you have done well before, then the first tee shot will become an action from reaction. When having trouble getting off the first tee it's best to change your disappointment to your own advantage that could develop into a different outlook on the golf round ahead. Attempt to swing at eighty percent with one key thought preferably (solid contact) rather than smash and slash. After a few holes momentum and aggressiveness will increase from confidence gained after playing in the middle of the green fairway. Just be patient enough to perform every golf swing to the best of your ability. Don't allow any outside or inner distractions interfere with the physical perfection of the flow like poetry in motion.

One of the most unanswered questions in golf is how do you maintain the momentum in the golf zone or when everything I do during a round of golf gels together? The zone of unknown performance is caused by just letting it happen without force. The feeling is that nothing can go wrong while every shot is struck closer to the flag with little effort. On the green the regulation hole becomes the size of a bucket in your mind.

Your golf swing becomes a well oiled machine that separates its self from mind concentration needed to put the ball in the hole. Striking the golf ball for the best opportunities that becomes endless on the green and make-able from any distance. What a feeling. If every round of golf could be similar then golf would become much easier to understand and the frustration level would diminish. Unfortunately, great golf only lasts for the round and tomorrow becomes a new day where anything could happen out of the zone that would certainly challenge your potential to shoot that low score again.

Most birdies made by professional tour players are on par five's that simply result from the exceptional distances the golf ball is hit that turns the longer holes into a normal par fours. The golf course becomes a par sixty eight before the tour player starts the round at most tournament stops. When I speak of a tour player in the zone is usually from their play on the par three's and tricky par four holes while knocking off half a dozen birdies rather than the expected birdies on par five holes. The momentum is in full in score mode to card an incredible low score for the day. Now that you just made a birdie the question is how to get the next one and another after that? There is a strong belief that everything you do is magical and if you demonstrate some swag your swagger would increase. Walk the walk and do the talk if a talkative personality. Even if laid back by nature is your make-up, you still would be walking like a peacock from being excited and enthusiastic. Of course you could hit the golf ball in close and have a wonderful opportunity with a possible near miss to end your birdie streak. However, that never really enters your mind as long as a positive mental attitude is maintained.

Momentum is increased with increased confidence. You have done this before so you see it and you make it happen with clear vision. Whether it be the golf gods or God Almighty looking down favourably on your golf round there is an undisputed reason why this is happening to enhance performance. When momentum is in your favour and expectations are high don't upset the apple cart by bringing any negative thoughts to disrupt your calm emotional state. To maintain the birdie fest while in the golf zone will require the necessary patience to remain with concentration of one shot at a time. The golfer's next shot should eliminate difficulty and provide more opportunity to free wheel with a good attitude and open mind. Believe and you will achieve when you manage your game as a positive golfer.

ABOUT THE AUTHOR

For over fifty years I have been dedicated toward striking the golf ball in an attempt to become one of the most knowledgeable on the golf swing worldwide. My exclusive interaction with great Canadian ball strikers far exceeds the general instructional information passed back and forth amongst many golf instructors or golf analysts. I know how to consistently put the golf club face on the golf ball square to hit the golf ball straight. I also have the ability to pick-out the hidden things in the golf swing other golf instructors are unaware of. Unfortunately, the rightful recognition was never provided to this author/instructor in an attempt to protect some of the so called golf geniuses in the lime light that only think they know.

My Ten Definitive Golf Lessons will complete the Finish to the Sky series. Hopefully, many more golfers will be able to obtain all three books that will help all golfers achieve some of their golfing goals.

At age sixty three I still face unwanted health issues from a severe heart attack that almost took my life in 2014. With continued exercise I hope to create some recent videos pertaining to the golf instruction displayed in the Finish to the Sky series. It becomes paramount that any golf instruction obtained from my books or future videos will contribute toward building a much more repetitive golf swing for the average player. Tour players are welcome to contact me if their desire is to learn how to hit the golf ball pure and straight.

With credentials as a University/College graduate I have utilized my education to author golf books from my personal instructional experience. Achievement of a black belt in Chito Ryu karate in 2002 is a style that originated in Okinawa south of Japan. The martial arts have become useful for flexibility and mind control that I have incorporated into advanced instruction with relation to golf. The mind and body must work in balance and cooperation with each other. I have promoted identification of these similarities for years in order to play great golf and strike the golf ball consistently straight down the fairway on a daily basis.

It was my thinking that any contribution of knowledge to inform the world needed individuality rather than to agree with the rest of the pack for social trait acceptance. I am sorry if I offended anyone by not being the outgoing social butterfly. It was absolutely necessary to protect this historical information during the publication process of each book, particularly to ensure those exclusive golf secrets never got into the wrong hands. However, I welcome constructive criticism along with your enthusiasm or support for the only golf swing I teach. Why would I teach any other golf swing when I learned from the greatest ball striker in the world for many years?

Regards,

Greg Lavern
Canadian Golf Author/Master Golf Instructor

ABOUT THE AUTHOR
ILLUSTRATION – GREG LAVERN

Author Greg Lavern Charlottetown PEI Canada

GREG LAVERN
IRON SWING SERIES

Set-up
Bend from the waist with weight on heels and inside the insteps.

61

Take-a-way
Stretch back while still looking at the back of the golf ball.
This will allow the right hip to turn out of the way for fuller
rotation of the hips and shoulders. The older guys need this.

Top of back swing

The left arm goes across the chest on the back swing which enables the golf club to find the proper swing plane regardless of your body shape. You now have the major ingredient that gives you automatic on plane success.

Vertical drop The left palm of the hand and arm pushes vertically downward to the right heel on the transition.

Angle of attack
The club head is so last and lags behind so the heel of the
club head leads into pre-impact with the angle of attack
retained before the club head squares up naturally.

Impact moment Of truth
Right arm is relaxed and always under the left. The left arm
is the leader and forms one straight line from club head to
the top of left shoulder.

Extension of both arms
Hit through the golf ball and extend your club path for a
much longer extension of the arms down the line.

Shoulders Rotate

As the stomach turns to the target returns the club shaft
To an original starting plane from when the transition
previously changed the club shaft into an entirely
different and lower swing plane.

Finish to the Sky
Watching the flight of the golf ball while in balance
with control of my golf ball.

FINISH TO THE SKY
VOLUME THREE
My Ten Definitive Golf Lessons

DISCLAIMER

The author of this book has no affiliation or collaboration on golf instruction in anyway whatsoever with the Moe Norman Estate, Todd Graves, Todd Graves Golf School LLC, or the Natural Golf Company. The literary content and excellent illustrations in this book are based on the author's own golf swing with pictures taken during October 2017 at age sixty two. While nursing a heart attack with only thirty percent breathing capacity since 2014 certainly has become a challenge. The Authentic Tournament Winning Golf Swing is the true Moe Norman swing personally taught to the author in 1974, thirty years before the death of Moe Norman in 2004.

The individual, organization and companies named as non-affiliates hold zero authority and ownership over the author or this book. Their promotion of the Single Plane Swing or Natural Golf's Single Axis Swing previously used as marketing tools has nothing to do with how Moe Norman actually performed his personal golf swing or his own approach toward striking a golf ball during the era the author was taught. Moe Norman dropped the golf club on an entirely different plane during transition and wanted to be as low as he could through the hitting area. This combination easily changes the swing plane. Moe Norman would say, "the lower the better."

In crystal clear terms my authorship is based on my golf swing that Moe Norman taught the author from personal experience which is displayed in this book, FINISH TO THE SKY Volume Three My Ten Definitive Golf Lessons.

The author does not promote or believe in the Single Plane Swing or Natural Golf's Single Axis Swing based on the author's own personal experiences from a lengthy golf relationship where expert knowledge was passed down. For many years the author of this book practiced and played golf with Moe Norman learning his Authentic Tournament Winning Golf Swing. The Single Plane Swing and Single Axis Swing Plane were never mentioned and was not in Moe Norman's vocabulary during any of our numerous conversations. The last tournament win that was officially recorded on Moe Norman was 1987, years before these non-affiliates ever surfaced.

This disclaimer was important to let the reader know that you won't find any mystical Single Plane Swing or Single Axis Swing in this incredible book.

Thank you for ordering Volume Three!

Sincerely,

Greg Lavern
The Author

CLASSIC

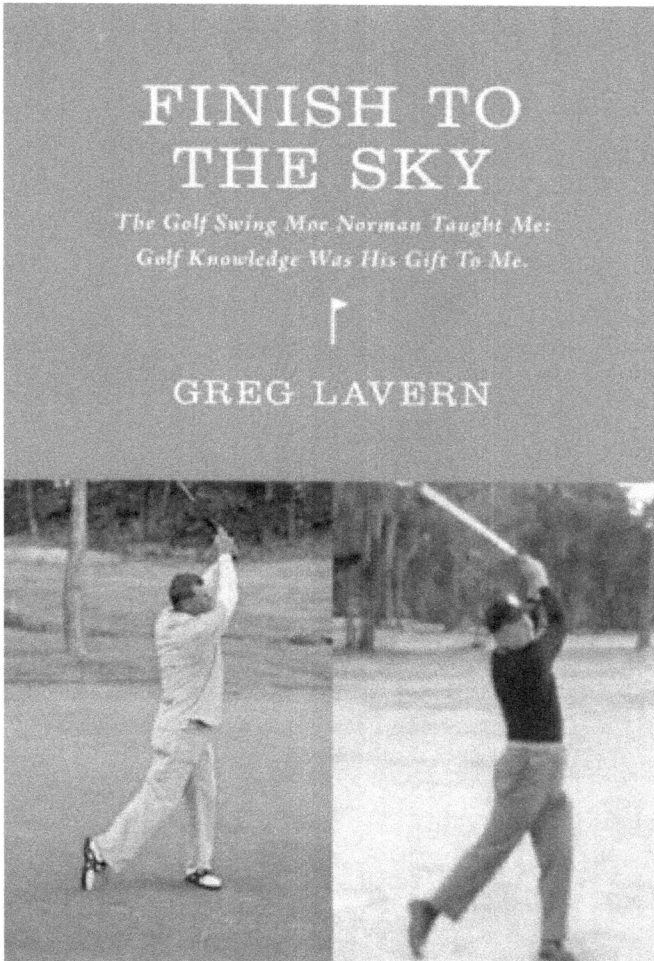

My first book in the Finish to the Sky Series

AUTHENTIC

FINISH TO THE SKY

*The Authentic Tournament Winning Golf
Swing Of Canadian Master Ball Striker
Moe Norman, I Personally Experienced.*

VOLUME TWO

GREG LAVERN

Author of FINISH TO THE SKY
The Golf Swing Moe Norman Taught Me:
Golf Knowledge Was His Gift To Me

Volume Two of the Finish to the Sky Series

73